The Mommy & Me Cookbook

By
Jamie Mayes
&
Lee Antwine, III

Edited by: Ruby Boston
Photography by: Tiera McMillan
Copyright © 2019 Jamie Mayes & Lee Antwine, III
All rights reserved.
ISBN-13: 978-0-578-51273-0

After a long day of work and school, I sometimes find it challenging to schedule quality time each evening with the sunshine of my life, my son. One thing all moms know is that a good dinner is important after such a long day, so I always try to cook meals I know Lee will enjoy. At first, I would routinely go to the kitchen and begin preparing dinner. Lee wanted to help and begged to get his little chair so he could stand next to me in the kitchen. I gave Lee small tasks like pouring the berries or being the "Stir Leader." Eventually, he started suggesting foods he liked as part of meals and for new recipes! What started as an evening responsibility for mom, turned into one of our favorite pastimes. As a mother, I especially enjoy cooking with Lee because it means healthier choices and great food adventures. Lee enjoys cooking because he feels as if he is a "big boy" when he can help mom. Most importantly, Lee and I both enjoy good food!

However, this book is not just about good food; it is about celebrating the beauty of motherhood and the bond between mothers and their children. It is a closer look at intimate family time and realizing how important it is to slow down our busy schedules to enjoy those precious moments we can never get again with our children. During our time in the kitchen, Lee and I have had some of our best conversations, some of our most serious learning moments and laughter we will never forget.

In *The Mommy & Me Cookbook*, we share some of our favorite meals and why they are so special to us. Using plenty of fresh fruits and veggies, we make healthy fun meals and snacks! We hope you and your child can enjoy creating great foods and memories in the kitchen just as much as we do!

LEE'S INTERVIEW WITH MOM

Q: Lee, what's your favorite food?

A: Salad.

Q: What's your favorite food to cook with mom?

A: Pancakes and waffles and sausage and eggs.

Q: What's your favorite snack?

A: Raspberries!

Q: Why do you like cooking with mom?

A: 'Cause I like you. And I like to cook.

Q: Do you remember the first food you and I cooked together?

A: Yes! Cookies with chocolate chips!

Q: What's your favorite hobby?

A: School. My school's name is… and I love it.

(He begged me to include his school's name, but I told him we could not.)

Q: What do you want to be when you grow up?

A: I wanna be nice!

The Mommy & Me Cookbook
RECIPES

Mom, this is a great opportunity to teach your toddler how to crack an egg. It may take a little practice, but they can master it. It also makes them feel a little independent when they crack the egg while you use the toaster. You can also let your toddler remove the food items and place them on the plate used to prep the meal. They will feel very engaged without handling knives or working near the hot stove.

When I first started making this breakfast, I used maple syrup. My son would eat most of it; however, he would often leave some of the waffle on his plate. One day, I ran out of maple syrup, but I had a jar of apple jelly, which I used for biscuits. I decided to try it on the waffles without telling Lee. It was an automatic hit, and he never wanted syrup on his waffles again. He nicknamed it "The Mickey Mouse Breakfast."

Mickey Mouse Breakfast for Two

Ingredients:

3 eggs
2 three-inch pieces of sausage
2 Mickey Mouse shaped waffles
1 tablespoon water
Cooking spray

Butter
Apple jelly
Salt
Pepper

Instructions:

Eggs

Crack 3 eggs into a bowl. Sprinkle them with salt and pepper. Whisk the eggs until they are light and fluffy. Place a skillet on low heat. Spray the skillet with cooking spray. When the skillet is hot, pour the eggs in and stir them constantly so they can cook evenly. When the eggs are almost completely cooked, turn the stove off and remove them from the heat. The eggs will continue to cook until they are just right. Divide the eggs and put them on two plates.

Waffles

Put two Mickey Mouse waffles into the toaster. Allow them to cook until they are a light golden brown. Place one waffle on each plate. Spread ½ teaspoon butter on each waffle while it is hot so the butter can melt. *(Mickey Mouse waffles can be found at the local grocery store. Mickey Mouse-shaped cookie cutters can be found online.)*

Fried Sausage

Cut each sausage down the center so that it is split into 2 long halves. Place both sausages into the skillet with the open center down. Allow the sausages to cook and sizzle until a light brown crust forms on the edges. Then, turn the sausages over so they can cook on the back. Pour 1 teaspoon water into the skillet to help the sausages brown evenly. When the water has disappeared, check the back of the sausages to see if they also have a light brown crust down the center. Turn the stove off and put one sausage on each plate.

Waffle Topping

Scoop 1 tablespoon apple jelly onto each waffle. Spread the jelly evenly to cover the waffle. Pour two glasses of orange juice and enjoy breakfast!

Mom, your child can help place the berries in the container and learn how to smash them. Though it may get a little messy, it is tons of fun for your child. Using safe utensils, your little one may also enjoy learning how to spread the food on the bread.

I started making this toast as a quick way to prepare breakfast for myself each morning. Dressing a toddler, feeding him, and getting out of the door on time can be challenging. However, this quick recipe takes less than five minutes. It is delicious, healthy, and filling. As parents, we cannot enjoy a good thing without our children insisting they try, too. Lee tried the toast, and he loved it! Now, it's a regular breakfast option for both of us. I usually pair the super fruity toast with two boiled eggs, which are cooked on Sunday nights and stored in the refrigerator throughout the week.

Super Fruity Toast

Ingredients:

1 slice wheat bread
1 tablespoon organic raw honey
1 tablespoon peanut butter
1/2 banana
½ cup blueberries, raspberries, or chopped strawberries
(or a mix of all three!)

Instructions:

First, toast the wheat bread in the toaster until it is evenly browned. Next, spread 1 tablespoon peanut butter onto the toast. Then, measure ½ cup blueberries, raspberries or chopped strawberries. Slice ½ banana into smaller pieces. Pour the berries and bananas into a small bowl. Use a fork to smash the fruit until they are broken into lumps. Scoop the berry and banana compote onto the toast on top of the peanut butter. Measure 1 tablespoon honey and drizzle it on top of the berry and banana compote. Spoiler alert: You and your little one might get addicted to this delicious breakfast treat!

Mom, give your child the title of "Stir Leader." He or she will be responsible for stirring the food to blend the macaroni- this is an important role! Yes, you can have more than one Stir Leader. In addition, there is no such thing as stirring too much for this recipe. Keep an eye on them near the stove, but let them have fun!

Like so many kids, mac n' cheese is one of Lee's favorites! He believes it can be paired with anything, and it is requested at least twice a week. If he is having a tough day, I know that Mama's Mac n' Cheese is the perfect pick-me-up. Here is our quick, easy and flavorful recipe!

Mama's Mac n' Cheese

Ingredients:

(1) 16 oz. bag of elbow macaroni noodles
½ cup heavy cream
½ medium-sized orange
1/3 teaspoon minced garlic
1/3 block white or yellow Velveeta cheese
½ cup mild cheddar cheese
3 tablespoons butter
½ teaspoon salt
2 tablespoons olive oil

Instructions:

Macaroni Noodles

Turn the stove on medium heat. Bring 4 cups water, 1 teaspoon salt, and 2 tablespoons olive oil to a rapid boil. When the water is bubbling, add the bag of large macaroni noodles. Allow them to cook for about ten minutes, stirring occasionally so the noodles do not stick together. When the noodles are soft, but not completely soft, turn the stove off. Get the colander and drain the noodles and water over the sink.

Prepping the Sauce

Chop 1/3 Velveeta cheese log into 1-inch blocks. Use a cheese grater to shave 1/2 cup mild cheddar cheese. Measure 1 cup heavy cream. Measure 3 tablespoons butter. Measure a ½ teaspoon minced garlic. Squeeze the juice of ½ an orange into a glass.

Combining the Mixture

Turn the stove onto low heat. Put the three tablespoons of butter into the pot. Allow the butter to begin to melt. Pour the macaroni noodles into the pot. Stir the mixture to coat the noodles with the butter. Pour ½ cup heavy cream into the pot. Add the Velveeta cheese. Once it begins to melt, add the cheddar cheese. Stir the mixture, making sure to stir all contents at the bottom of the pot. Add the minced garlic and orange juice. Stir the contents again. Put a top over the macaroni and cheese and allow it to simmer for about five minutes. Stir repeatedly to ensure the mac n' cheese does not stick to the pot. Turn the stove off. Serve the macaroni alongside a protein like chicken and a vegetable like our "Great Green Bean Delight!"

Mom, when using this recipe, your child can begin learning about measuring and counting while cooking. Help your child identify the correct number of items and teach them how to identify the correct measuring utensils. Now, they are applying what they may be learning at school into home activities.

Lee's favorite vegetable is green beans! Though he loves green beans from nearly anywhere, this green bean recipe is one of his favorite requests! Put a scoop next to his macaroni and watch an empty plate appear. I decided to share this same recipe at a family holiday gathering, and it was so successful that it is still one of my most requested dishes. Maybe it will become a favorite for your family, too.

Great Green Bean Delight

Ingredients:

(1) 8 oz. can green beans
2 strips bacon
¼ small onion
½ small orange
½ teaspoon minced garlic
2 tablespoons brown sugar
½ teaspoon salt
¼ teaspoon pepper

Instructions:

Cut the orange in half, squeeze the juice into a small container, and set it aside. Dice ¼ an onion into small pieces. Cut 2 strips bacon into small pieces. Put the items aside.

Place a small skillet on medium heat. When it is warm, pour the pieces of bacon into the skillet. When the bacon begins cooking, add the onions. Allow the onions and bacon to cook until the bacon is slightly crisp. Turn the skillet off. Place a small pot on medium heat. Pour the can of green beans into the pot. Add ¼ teaspoon salt and ¼ teaspoon pepper; allow the mixture to cook until it begins to simmer. Add 2 tablespoons brown sugar, ½ teaspoon minced garlic and juice from the orange. Stir the mixture. Add in the bacon and onions. Stir again. Turn the heat down to a low simmer and allow the mixture to cook for ten minutes, stirring occasionally. Turn the heat off and serve the "Great Green Bean Delight" as a side to your favorite meal!

Mom, of course, frying chicken is risky, but there are great ways your little one can help. As the Stir Leader, your child can stir the seasonings into the egg mixture and into the flour mixture. Little ones often love getting their hands dirty, so let your child dip the chicken into the egg and into the flour.

Although Lee loves his chicken baked or fried, I found him frequently asking for chicken from fast food restaurants. My first-time frying chicken for him was just after he turned four years old. He ate a first piece and then a second. Lee still enjoys baked chicken, but when he asks for fried chicken, this recipe is a winner!

Mama's Magnificent Fried Chicken

Ingredients:

(1) 8-10 pack chicken legs or wings
2 cups all-purpose flour
1 teaspoon baking powder
2 eggs
Canola cooking oil
Any type of Louisiana style seasoning salt

Instructions:

Rinse the chicken legs or wings and put them on a paper towel to drain. Mix 2 whisked eggs and 1 ½ tablespoons Louisiana seasoning salt in a large bowl. Put the chicken into the bowl with the seasoned eggs. Mix them together so the chicken is well coated with the seasoned eggs. Cover the bowl and put it to the side.

Turn the stove on medium and fill a deep skillet halfway with canola cooking oil. Pour 2 cups all-purpose flour in a separate bowl. Add 1 tablespoon Louisiana style seasoning salt. Add 1 teaspoon baking powder. Stir the mixture with a whisk or fork to evenly distribute the seasoning and baking powder throughout the flour. Take the chicken from the egg mixture and put it into the flour mixture one piece at a time. Cover the bowl and shake it gently so that the flour completely coats each piece of chicken.

Check to see if the grease is hot. (This can be done by adding a sprinkle of flour into the pot. If it sizzles, the oil is ready.) Gently lay pieces of chicken into the grease, allowing enough space for each piece to lie at the bottom. Allow the chicken to fry for 3 minutes; then turn it over. Allow the chicken to cook 3 for more minutes. To ensure the chicken is cooked thoroughly, poke it with a fork or knife near the part of the chicken that is the thickest. If the chicken drains a pinkish liquid, allow it to cook for another 2 minutes on each side. When the chicken has begun to float, remove it from the pot and put it into a colander or on paper towels to drain.

Mom, because of the many different ingredients in this recipe, your child will enjoy adding them into the bowl. The two of you can discuss the colors of the apples, grapes and cilantro, using this as a learning opportunity. When your Stir Leader combines all ingredients, a little excitement may ensue.

I refer to myself as a chicken salad connoisseur. If chicken salad is on the menu, I want to see what the flavor is about! I always classified chicken salad as an adult food, and I love whipping it up for friends. The combination of flavors was certainly something I did not think a toddler would enjoy. While sitting in front of the television one day, Lee picked up one of my crackers and dug up his own scoop of chicken salad. "I like this, Mama!" he said with his mouth full. Now, the chicken salad is a regular mom and son favorite in our house!

Chillin' with Mom Chicken Salad

Ingredients:

1 whole rotisserie chicken
2 boiled eggs
1 medium sized apple
10 purple grapes
2 sprigs cilantro
½ cups mayonnaise
1 stalk celery (optional)
½ teaspoon salt
¼ teaspoon pepper
½ teaspoon garlic salt

Instructions:

Remove all chicken from between the skin and bones of the rotisserie chicken. Chop into small chunks and place into a medium-sized bowl. Chop the eggs into small pieces. Add them to the chicken. Remove the skin from the apple; cut the apple from around the core. Dice the apple into small pieces. Add it to the mixture. Cut the grapes in half. Then, slice each half into three sections. Slice the three sections in half. Add the chopped grapes into the bowl. Stir the mixture. Then, pour ½ cup mayonnaise into the bowl. Stir the mixture until the mayonnaise fully coats the salad. Add the salt, pepper, and garlic salt. Stir again, mixing the seasonings into the salad. Finely chop the leaves of the cilantro and add them to the salad. (Optional: Cut the celery stalk in half and dice it into small pieces. Add the pieces to the salad for a fresh crunchiness.)

The chicken salad pairs well with Ritz crackers, which are Lee's favorite "spoon" for this recipe!

Mom, there are various roles your child can assume in this recipe. From placing the butter in the pan before it goes into the oven to draining the corn or being the Stir Leader, they can be a great help. Do not be afraid to let them make a little mess while learning!

Lee's love for bread is genetic! Whether it's rolls, slices, breadsticks or cornbread, we get a little giddy when we see bread. To ramp up traditional cornbread, I decided to add a little kick. Now, Lee and I indulge in this deliciousness on the side of warm winter dishes or as a slightly sweet snack. Let me tell you a secret- you can't eat just one piece!

Lee's Creamy Cheese Cornbread

Ingredients:

2 boxes cornbread mix
(1) 14.75 oz. can whole kernel corn
(1) ½ 14.75 oz. can cream corn
1 cup shredded mild cheddar cheese
2 tablespoons melted butter

Instructions:

Preheat the oven as instructed on the cornbread mix package. Mix the cornbread using the ingredients required according to the box. Drain the can of whole kernel corn. Add the whole kernel corn and half a can of creamed corn into the cornbread mixture. Stir together. Add 1 cup shredded mild cheddar cheese and stir the mixture again. Set the mixture aside. Spoon 2 tablespoons melted butter into an 8x8 inch baking dish; pour the cornbread mixture into the dish. Place it into the preheated oven and allow it to cook until it is golden brown. Spread butter on top of the hot cornbread. Cut the cornbread into squares and serve alongside lunch or dinner. When served alone, it makes a great snack!

Mom, your little one may enjoy crunching up the graham crackers while you chop the pecans. Do not forget- your fearless Stir Leader is always needed!

I discovered my son's love for this recipe by accident. We were having Juneteenth dinner, and I put a small scoop of yams on his plate, thinking he would not like them. However, the sugary flavor of these potatoes attacked his little taste buds, and he ate three servings! Though it is usually a holiday treat, I know he will clean his plate and ask for seconds when I make Yes Ma'am Yams!

Yes Ma'am Yams

Ingredients:

(1) 29 oz. can yams
2 graham cracker planks
2 tablespoons butter
¾ cup brown sugar
½ teaspoon cinnamon
1 teaspoon vanilla extract
1 small orange
1 cup pecans

Instructions:

The Yams

Squeeze the juice from the orange into a cup. Drain half the juice from the can of yams. Pour the yams into the pot and turn the stove on medium heat. As the yams cook, add ¾ cup brown sugar, the juice from the small orange, ½ teaspoon cinnamon and 1 teaspoon vanilla extract. Turn the pot down to a low simmer and allow the ingredients to cook together, stirring occasionally. Add ¼ cup butter. Allow the yams to simmer until they began to fall apart.

The Topping

Chop the pecans into small pieces. Crush the graham into small chunks. Place a small skillet on low heat and add the remaining butter. Once the butter is melted, add the brown sugar and the graham crackers. Allow the mixture to cook until it turns into a crumble-like texture.

Scoop the yams into a bowl. Add the graham cracker and pecan topping on top of the yams. Enjoy as a side or as a dessert. It also tastes great with a scoop of vanilla ice cream.

Mom, this is a hot water recipe, but do not be nervous. Your little one can help with adding brown sugar and honey. With your supervision, your child can also add the tea bags; they are often amazed when watching the color of the water change! This is also a good time to talk with your little one about the dangerous areas in the kitchen that they should never touch without an adult present.

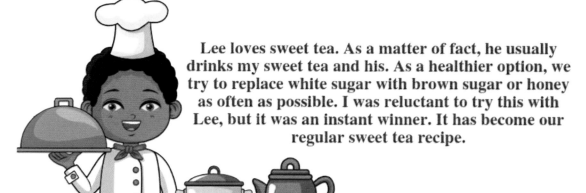

Lee loves sweet tea. As a matter of fact, he usually drinks my sweet tea and his. As a healthier option, we try to replace white sugar with brown sugar or honey as often as possible. I was reluctant to try this with Lee, but it was an instant winner. It has become our regular sweet tea recipe.

Lee's Lemon Tea

Ingredients:

1 gallon water
1 lemon
1 cup brown sugar
¾ cup honey
2 tea bags

Instructions:

Turn a pot on medium heat. Pour 1/3 gallon of water into the pot and bring it to a boil. In a separate larger pot, pour the remaining water. While waiting on the water to boil, cut the lemon in half and then into small slices. Measure 1 cups brown sugar and ¾ cup honey.

Once the 1/3 gallon water begins to boil, add two tea bags to the hot water. Turn the boiling pot off and allow the tea bags to soak in the hot water for three minutes. Pour the hot water and tea mixture of the water into a pitcher. Add the brown sugar and honey to the tea. Stir the mixture until the sugar dissolves. Add the remaining 2/3 gallon water to the pitcher. Stir until the water and tea mixture are well blended. Cut the lemon in half. Squeeze the juice from ½ lemon into the tea. Slice the other half of the lemon into small pieces. Add them to the tea so that the lemon juice will continue to slowly release into the tea. Allow the tea to cool on the counter. Fill a cup with ice and pour Lee's Sweet Lemon Tea over the ice. After an hour, the remaining tea can be placed into the refrigerator to serve later.

Mom, this is a great opportunity to teach your child to measure and count berries. The child can also add the sugar. They can still be the Stir Leader, but your support may be needed to keep balance between the child and the drinking pitcher.

Before I had Lee, one of my favorite pastimes was experimenting with fresh fruits and veggies. I began making my fresh fruit punches during the summer; however, when I had Lee, it seemed easier to just grab something from the shelf. Since he has gotten older, we have been able to make the punches together. Last summer, we made our first fruit punch using two of his favorite berries. Not only are they delicious as a drink, they can also be turned into homemade popsicles! Our Family Fresh Blue-Blackberry Punch is a refreshing hit with Lee and me!

Family Fresh Blue-Blackberry Punch

Ingredients:

(1) 6 oz. carton blueberries
(1) 12 oz. carton blackberries
2 medium lemons
2 cups sugar
1 ½ quarts water

Instructions:

Rinse the 6 ounce container of blueberries and ½ the container of blackberries thoroughly; place them aside on a paper towel. Place a wire strainer over the top of a drinking pitcher. Scoop a handful of blueberries into the strainer and use fingers to press the juice into the drinking pitcher; separate the juice of the berries from the flesh and seeds. Repeat the process until all blueberries have been pressed through the strainer. Rinse the strainer and empty the residue from the blueberries. Place the wire strainer back over the top of the pitcher. Repeat the process with the blackberries. Cut the lemons in half and scoop the seeds from them. Squeeze the juice from 1 ½ lemons into the pitcher of berry juice.

Add 2 cups sugar and pour 1 ½ quarts water into the juice mixture. Stir until the sugar dissolves. Allow the punch to chill in the refrigerator or serve over a glass of ice. The kids are sure to enjoy this natural fruit punch!

Mom, your child will enjoy every part of this activity. The child can count berries, pour them into the container, and be the Stir Leader. This activity provides a great chance for your child to achieve more independence and have fun.

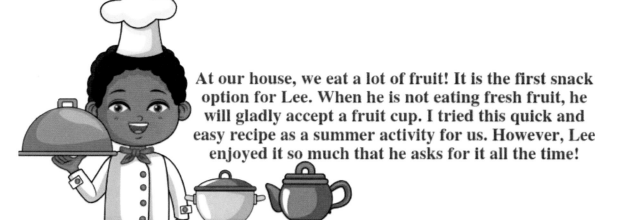

At our house, we eat a lot of fruit! It is the first snack option for Lee. When he is not eating fresh fruit, he will gladly accept a fruit cup. I tried this quick and easy recipe as a summer activity for us. However, Lee enjoyed it so much that he asks for it all the time!

Family Fruit Cups

Ingredients:

(1) 12 oz. container raspberries
(1) 12 oz. container blueberries
(1) 12 oz. container strawberries
(1) 12 oz. container blackberries
1/3 cup honey
2 small oranges
6 small storage cups or bowls

Instructions:

Rinse the strawberries and chop them into fourths. Pour them into a dish large enough for all fruits. Pour the raspberries, blueberries, and blackberries into a colander and rinse them thoroughly. Drain them and pour the fruits in with the strawberries. Cut the oranges in half and squeeze the juice into the bowl of fruit. Add a ½ cup honey to the fruit mixture and stir so that the honey coats all fruits evenly.

Scoop the fruit into the cups or bowls so that the fruit is evenly distributed into each cup. Cover the snack cups and place them in the refrigerator to cool. This can be served as a healthy but delicious snack for the kids. Freezing the fruit cups will not only make them last longer, it will be quite refreshing on a hot summer day.

Mom, your child can assist by adding the ingredients for this simple recipe. In addition, someone must lay out the crackers, and your little one is the perfect person to do so. You and your child can do nearly everything together for this recipe.

This was an experimental recipe I tried when I started writing this book. Lee loves peanut butter crackers, and I often tell him I think he is a little old man at heart. We keep at least two packages in the pantry. However, one day, I wondered what would happen if I made peanut butter crackers from scratch. So, I did. There's only one problem: I think I love these even more than my child does.
Thanks, Lee!

Homemade Peanut Butter Crackers

Ingredients:

¾ cup peanut butter
½ cup powdered sugar
½ teaspoon vanilla extract
2 tablespoons milk
1 sleeve Ritz crackers

Instructions:

Pour ¾ cup peanut butter into a bowl. Stir or blend it until it is smooth and creamy. Add ½ cup powdered sugar. Stir or blend until the powdered sugar completely disappears. Add ½ teaspoon vanilla extract and mix. Add 2 tablespoons milk to smooth the texture of the mixture.

Lay half of the sleeve of Ritz crackers on a plate or cutting board. Spoon the peanut butter mixture onto each cracker. Add the remaining crackers on top of the peanut butter to make the sandwiches complete. Allow your mini taste-testers to enjoy the snack with their favorite drink!

ABOUT THE AUTHORS

Jamie Mayes is an author, speaker, and teacher who lives in Monroe, Louisiana. She has a bachelor's degree in English from Louisiana State University of Baton Rouge. She also has a master's degree in Secondary Education from the University of Louisiana at Monroe. She earned her Educational Specialist degree in Instructional Leadership from Northcentral University. She has been a teacher for eleven years, but her greatest passion is sharing the beauty of writing with all audiences. This Louisiana native has always had a passion for cooking and has been doing so since she was seven years old. She decided to bring the worlds of cooking, writing and motherhood together after the birth of her son, Lee, who also shares a love for cooking.

Lee is a bubbly four-year-old who spends his time enjoying school, playing with his toys, and talking to anyone who will listen. He is a Pre-K student who enjoys learning and doing schoolwork. One of his favorite pastimes is cooking with his mom. His joy for food and fun helped them create new recipes they both enjoy!

Made in the USA
Monee, IL
27 November 2020